Soul of Marseille

A GUIDE TO EXCEPTIONAL EXPERIENCES

WRITTEN BY EZÉCHIEL ZÉRAH

JONGLEZ PUBLISHING

Travel guides

'In this world,
there are two kinds of people:
the Marseillais
and those who wish they were.'

LIONEL TONINI

Marseille is not just the second city of France but a country in itself. This city is unlike any other and in recent years many of our visitors, domestic and international, have wished to know it better. But, unlike many other large regions in France, Marseille doesn't offer itself up for that. It's territory that we must learn to dig into, that calls for patience and how we look at other people more than any (rare) great architecture. This is how the fascination of Marseille reveals itself, with all its beauty, with all its flaws. A wonderful city for those who know how to watch and listen …

Nothing makes me happier than to 'show off' my city, where I've lived for 33 years, and to tell its story through places sometimes unknown to the residents themselves. And, even for places we think we know, already in the spotlight, I like to move the angle of view because there's always nuggets hidden within. Forget the bad reputation, dive in and lose yourself in the streets of Marseille. That's where much of the local action plays out.

Between two random forays, I've cooked up a 'best of' for you. Like holding a friendly hand. A list of 30 experiences is at once too short and at the same time enough to bite into this corner of the Mediterranean.

Bon voyage!

Ezéchiel Zérah, former editor-in-chief of the gastronomy pages of *L'Express*, was born in Marseille where he still lives. In 2023, Hachette published his first (big) book, *Marseille. Un jour sans faim !* (Marseille. A day without hunger!), which soon became the city's culinary reference. He works for national (*Le Monde M magazine*, *Les Echos Week-end*) and local publications (*Time Out Marseille*, *BFM Marseille TV*).

WHAT YOU WON'T FIND
IN THIS GUIDE

– info on the little tourist train that criss-crosses the city streets
– the Mucem (or not exactly)
– opening hours of the Bonne Mère (Catholic basilica of Notre-Dame-de-la-Garde)
– bouillabaisse (seafood stew) eateries at the Old Port

WHAT YOU WILL FIND
IN THIS GUIDE

– a pizzeria concealed behind a bar
– the biscuit shop where insiders go
– a café where you can feel the pulse of the city
– an unknown island
– a legendary fruit juice
– breathtaking hotel rooms
– the 'best restaurant in the South'
– Marseille's favourite whipped cream
– treasures from the oldest hardware store in France

SYMBOLS OF
MARSEILLE

less than
10 euros

from
10 to 40 euros

more than
40 euros

in the
city centre

most
beautiful view

reservation
recommended

Opening times often vary,
so we recommend checking them directly
on the website of the place you plan to visit.

30 EXPERIENCES

01. Where to have breakfast?
02. Sleep like an emperor
03. A snack on the roof terrace of a rowing club
04. Discover the best *navette* in Marseille
05. Discover the city's most vibrant markets
06. Future kitchen stars
07. Italy at the table
08. Better than a ceramics workshop
09. Dine in a boutique or with a visiting chef
10. A snapshot of Marseille, facing the beach
11. The best restaurant in the south?
12. All of Provence in a little-known museum
13. The Marseillais also love whipped cream and red meat
14. Juice from a legendary local kiosk
15. The best picnic in town
16. Dive into the storerooms of the Mucem
17. Art by appointment
18. Marseille, pizza capital of France
19. Lunch at the farm
20. A meal in the calanques
21. Hike up to the most beautiful vantage point in the calanques
22. High-flying drinks scene
23. Taste the overseas territories
24. Celebrating the sea
25. Faïence in a museum
26. Head out to meet some street vendors
27. In the footsteps of Marcel Pagnol
28. Rooms with a view
29. Discover a little-known island
30. Marseille's most beautiful view

WHERE TO HAVE BREAKFAST?

One of the pleasures of life is breakfast at the café. Whether you're from Marseille or a B&B tourist, we all need somewhere to relax with morning coffee and the papers.

For a real coffee in a classic bistro, just go down the famous monumental staircase at Saint-Charles station and carry on left for 10 minutes to reach **Comptoir Dugommier**.

COMPTOIR DUGOMMIER
14, BOULEVARD DUGOMMIER
13001 MARSEILLE

+339 50 12 32 62

comptoirdugommier.fr

Or else walk through the door of **Café de la Banque**, next to Marseilles prefecture, to order a *café-verre* (espresso that comes in a glass rather than a cup) from the friendliest bistro owner in the city, Arnaud Lafargue.

In the chic and quiet Vauban district, on the heights of the Phocaean city (so-called because Marseille was founded by Greek sailors from Phocaea, now in Turkey), modernists will rush to **Carlotta With**, a high-ceilinged deli famous for its *pompe* (local brioche made with olive oil), plain or chocolate-flavoured, and its homemade coconut yoghurt.

 CAFÉ DE LA BANQUE
24, BOULEVARD PAUL PEYTRAL
13006 MARSEILLE

+334 91 33 35 07
lecafedelabanque.fr

 CARLOTTA WITH
84, BOULEVARD VAUBAN
13006 MARSEILLE

+339 70 66 98 18
Instagram: @Carlotta With

MAISON JOURNO

You might prefer a Tunisian-style breakfast at **Maison Journo**, with its blue storefront that's been here since the early 1960s. Roger Journo (1930–2022) was the figurehead of this Tunisian bakery known for its *oreillettes* ('light as a veil', as they used to say), sublime almond macaroons (called *guizadas*), its fresh rose loukoum (Turkish delight) and delectably flaky gazelle horns (crescent-shaped almond cookies). Pastries 'guaranteed until you leave!' in Roger's throw-away line to his customers. His grandson David has taken over the family tradition, and from 9 in the morning he serves lemonade with the granita texture known all over town. To feel like one of the locals, try dipping a *boulou* (dry almond biscuit) in it.

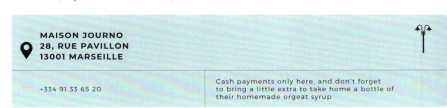

MAISON JOURNO
28, RUE PAVILLON
13001 MARSEILLE

+334 91 33 65 20

Cash payments only here, and don't forget to bring a little extra to take home a bottle of their homemade orgeat syrup

SLEEP LIKE
AN EMPEROR

We no longer showcase the famous Maison Empereur, the oldest hardware store in France, but we can say a word about the vast apartment (90 square metres) that can be booked for the night there. In our eyes, this is the most beautiful guest room in the city, located in the effervescent Noailles district, the real 'belly of Marseille'. Why? Decor that dives into the past with old tools and objects displayed everywhere like a cabinet of curiosities, with a copper bath, a magnificent bed in the living room and plenty of other surprises …

L'ARRIÈRE-BOUTIQUE
4, RUE DES RÉCOLETTES
13001 MARSEILLE

+339 70 19 43 06   unenuit@empereur.fr

A few words all the same on the store, a 'monument' established in 1770 as a blacksmith's shop before branching into trading. The Marseillais have all heard at least once: 'If the Emperor doesn't stock it, it's nowhere to be found.' So you can find everything (the old-style toyshop, for example, is a mini museum), including objects you won't see elsewhere.

Such as? *Poumié 3 pommes*, a type of 19th-century Provencal pottery used to bake apples – the little round dishes are good for serving mezze appetisers; an outdoor rug made from *scourtin* (filter for olive oil); a terracotta oven to make your own roasted garlic; a pea fork; or even a mushroom brush crafted from beechwood and horsehair ...

MAISON EMPEREUR
4, RUE DES RÉCOLETTES
13001 MARSEILLE

+334 91 54 02 29   empereur.fr

A SNACK ON THE ROOF TERRACE
OF A ROWING CLUB

Here's an insider's gem, perfectly located just a 15-minute walk from the iconic Old Port: a restaurant with an unparalleled view of the boat-lined harbour and Fort Saint-Jean, perched on the upper floors of a rowing club at the far end of the Rive Neuve quay. There's even a roof terrace above the restaurant that's perfect for enjoying a drink and good food – prepared by a chef who once helmed Le Peron, an institution just down the road.

Start with *panisses* (chickpea flour fritters), followed by fish gravlax paired with fruit, pickles and herb sauces, then round off your meal with a dessert from Depuichaffray – famous for its millefeuille, which reliably attracts the city's stars. The endearing Christian Ernst, chef and owner of the Rowing Club Restaurant since 1998, deserves a special mention. Like many Marseille natives, he's always quick with a joke – the better to hide his tender heart.

ROWING CLUB RESTAURANT
34, BOULEVARD CHARLES LIVON
13007 MARSEILLE

+334 91 90 07 78

rowingclubrestaurant.fr

DISCOVER THE BEST *NAVETTE* IN MARSEILLE

Marseille may not be known for its sweets, but there's one you really must try: the *navette*. This (very) dry, elongated biscuit flavoured with orange blossom is said to be a nod to the boats of the 'Saint Maries' who brought Christianity to Provence in the year 45. If you're looking to sample them, locals will point you to Four des Navettes – an iconic bakery dating back to the late 13th century, whose scent still fills the air of the neighbourhood – or José Orsoni's renowned Navettes des Accoules, a more recent take on the classic.

But there's a third option: Frédéric Dejuli, who was trained by his Corsican father, who himself learned from the legendary Orsoni. (Do you follow?) Charming and understated, Frédéric Dejuli's little shop is on the heights of the city, in the chic Bompard district far from the tourist crowds. Beyond his famed *navettes* and exquisite Corsican biscuits made with white wine or orange, Frédéric Dejuli has consistently proven himself, over our many visits, to be a master pastry chef. If you spot any gingerbread or *fiadone* (Corsica's version of cheesecake), definitely give them a try!

180° BISCUITERIE ARTISANALE
39, BOULEVARD BOMPARD
13007 MARSEILLE

Instagram: @180biscuiterie

DISCOVER THE CITY'S **MOST VIBRANT MARKETS**

On Wednesday mornings, the Farmers' Market on Cours Julien with its bohemian atmosphere is a must. Stroll through it to the rhythm of live music, inhaling the incomparable aroma of pizza that fills the air. Be sure to stop by the stalls of market gardener Jamal Benhida, who supplies the city's top young chefs, and Luc Falcot, renowned for his fresh, local Brousse du Rove goat's cheese.

And of course, we can't *not* mention the iconic fish market in the Old Port, open daily, where you can pick up fresh bonito (a tuna-like fish perfect for tartare) and 'eyes of Saint Lucia', small Corsican shellfish believed to bring good luck.

There are also two exceptional, ultra high-quality micro-markets, where you can have a bite to eat and something to drink while discovering new artisans each time you go: the Saint-Victor market, held on the last Sunday of every month, and La Vaubanette, named after the Vauban district in the hills above the Phocaean city.

MARCHÉ PAYSAN (FARMER'S MARKET) COURS JULIEN 13006 MARSEILLE	MARCHÉ SAINT-VICTOR 3, PLACE SAINT-VICTOR 13007 MARSEILLE	MARCHÉ LA VAUBANETTE
WED: 8am / 1pm	Last sunday of every month: 9am / 4pm Instagram: @marchesaintvictor.13	Place and date on Instagram: @lavaubanette

FUTURE
KITCHEN STARS

They don't yet have a Michelin star at the time of writing but they already deserve it!

> First of all, we mean **Belle de Mars**, a small restaurant not in a district known for its cuisine (La Joliette) but which alone attracts gourmets. This is the 'fault' of Michel Marini and his partner Kim-Mai Bui, both in the kitchen armed with solid gold CVs (Le Petit Nice in Marseille, Ze Kitchen Gallery and Lasserre in Paris …).

BELLE DE MARS
56, RUE DE FORBIN
13002 MARSEILLE

+339 86 57 24 58

belledemars.fr

> In the city centre, chef Edgar Bosquez from Panama is also a heavyweight, installed with his wife at **Ekume**. We fondly remember the *baudroie* (local name for monkfish) with chickpea stew, not surprising given the chef's passion for the sea and his excellent training (Bocuse, Le Petit Nice, Lucas Carton in Paris).

EKUME
139, RUE SAINTE
13007 MARSEILLE

+334 91 73 46 91

ekume-restaurant.com

© DIVINEMENCIEL

> He may be taciturn but the talent of the Venezuelan David Mijoba is in inverse proportion to to his chatter. When no one else makes their own *poutargue* (a local speciality made from dried mullet eggs), **Mijoba** sets to. Always where you least expect him, as with that choucroute served at lunch, so fine and elegant that it made us forget Alsace. A great gent who opened his creative kitchen on the heights of the city, along a pleasant shopping street in the chic district of Vauban.

MIJOBA
79, BOULEVARD VAUBAN
13006 MARSEILLE

+334 91 92 03 53

mijoba.fr

#07
ITALY
AT THE TABLE

Given the waves of immigration from across the Alps, you could almost say that the Marseillais are French-speaking Italians. Le Jambon de Parme – France's first Michelin-starred Italian restaurant, back in the 1930s – may no longer exist, but other dining spots are now carrying on that legacy with similar success. Here are a few examples ...

> **Atelier Renata**: Beware: this place takes charm to another level – of all places, right near the main Saint Charles railway station, in what is otherwise a culinary desert. Chef Erika Blu, a former musician, has converted an art dealer's flat into an exquisite restaurant with a *table d'hôte* menu, open three evenings a week. Here, the Roman-born chef introduces her guests (around a dozen, all gathered around the same table) to *cucina povera*, a cuisine that celebrates the alchemical transformation of leftovers. We were treated to a delightful cup of bread salad with tomato and olive oil, a slice of bread spread with a dark poultry-liver paste, poultry sausage and *pici* (very thick spaghetti) served with *ragù bianco* and *vino rosso*. Erika regularly invites mammas from Tuscany or Naples to come and cook here, keeping alive the memory of her grandmother, Renata, through the culinary traditions of her homeland.

ATELIER RENATA
2A, RUE GUY FABRE
13001 MARSEILLE

+339 79 02 97 15

Instagram: @atelier_renata_marseille

> **La Bastide de Massimo**: Even many locals don't know about this 18th-century bastide, which was transformed in 2014 into a chic guinguette-style restaurant. On the heights of the La Blancarde district, away from the city centre, its terrace is decorated with cheerful garlands and blossoming orange trees. We recommend the octopus with warm potatoes, the homemade schnitzel and gnocchi with comforting tomato sauce, and the exceptional hazelnut ice cream, imported directly from Italy.

> **A Moro**: Hands down the best Italian restaurant in the very centre of Marseille, this trattoria, launched by a young team in 2022, serves fresh pasta and an extremely competitive lunch menu.

> **La Cantinetta**: This Italian institution was opened almost two decades ago by an endearing Armenian with a deep love for all things Italian. Come for the pasta, the courtyard and the famous panettone French toast.

> **Jogging Trattoria**: Charming at night, this concept store turns into a cosy little city inn with grandma's white curtains, table-cloths, and candles everywhere. The chef, hailing from Lombardy, crafts comforting dishes like his Milanese cotoletta, looking like a giant fried chicken. Divine cooking inside!

  LA BASTIDE DE MASSIMO
30, RUE POUCEL
13004 MARSEILLE

+339 86 26 56 72

  A MORO
3, RUE VENTURE
13001 MARSEILLE

+337 65 80 37 37

© GUILLAUME MAUGAIN

LA CANTINETTA
24, COURS JULIEN
13006 MARSEILLE

+334 91 48 10 48
Instagram: @lacantinettamarseille

JOGGING TRATTORIA
104, RUE PARADIS
13006 MARSEILLE

+334 91 81 44 94
Instagram: @jogging_trattoria

35

BETTER THAN
A CERAMICS WORKSHOP

Poterie Ravel, founded in 1837, is renowned far beyond the Bouches-du-Rhône department for its elegant flower pots crafted in Aubagne, just 20 km east of Marseille.

At the turn of the last century, Aubagne was home to around 50 such factories, thanks to its proximity to rich clay soil and the Huveaune river.

Good news: every Thursday morning you can take a tour of the workshops. While there, you can also discover a period Provençal kitchen, as well as a small museum dedicated to pottery-making in Provence. The items on display include funerary objects, a brick bed warmer, a chicken waterer, a broom holder, a cockroach trap and even baby bottles.

The centre also organises exhibitions by contemporary artists in residence, who collaborate with Ravel.

POTERIE RAVEL
8, AVENUE DES GOUMS
13400 AUBAGNE

poterie-ravel.com   Instagram: @poterieravel

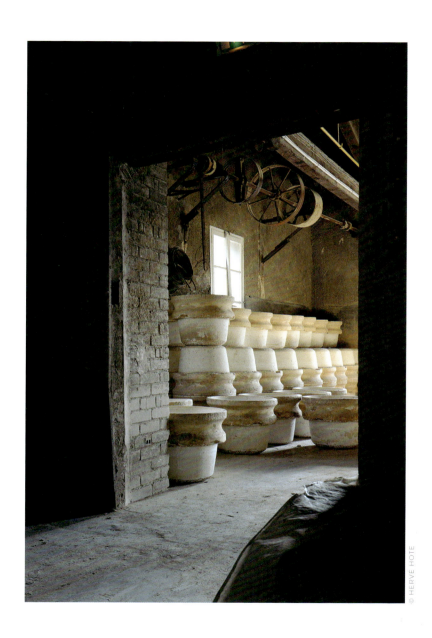

DINE IN A BOUTIQUE
OR WITH A VISITING CHEF

More and more places – and they're not even all restaurants – are embracing the concept of chefs in residence, a chance to discover multiple culinary identities. Among these are **Provisions** (a bookshop/café/canteen with a special focus on women), as well as **La Ola**, **Camas Sutra** and others.

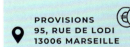

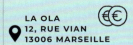

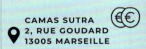

© AMANCIO AVIT

Restaurants that also regularly bring in colleagues from elsewhere include **Amo** (which doubles as an art gallery run by the vivacious Luciana Amado) and **Livingston** (co-owned by the highly acclaimed Top Chef 2024 candidate Valentin Raffali).

AMO 137, RUE SAINTE 13007 MARSEILLE		LIVINGSTON 5, RUE CRUDÈRE 13006 MARSEILLE	
+339 56 22 19 83 Instagram: @amo_marseille		livingstonmarseille.com	

A SNAPSHOT OF MARSEILLE,
FACING THE BEACH

Twenty minutes walk takes you from the Old Port to the first beach. Of course we're talking about the sandy Catalans beach. Fancy a coffee? **Le Welcome Café**, just behind, is a local harbour gem. You can ask for your espresso to go or stay on the spot to capture the essence of Marseillais chat surrounded by wall-to-wall mirrors. But never order a *pastis* – here you ask for a Ricard or a 51, straight or with orgeat (it's then a *mauresque* or 'Moorish'), mint (*perroquet* or 'parrot') or grenadine (*tomate* or 'tomato') syrups. We also like Le Welcome for Nathalie's kitchen on weekday lunchtimes (especially her impressive fish *rougaille*) and its extra-long opening hours (open all night, yes!).

LE WELCOME CAFÉ
8, RUE DES CATALANS
13007 MARSEILLE

Open 24/7

Not to mention two must-sees in the neighbourhood. First, **Chez Michel**, the best bouillabaisse in Marseille – expensive (90 euros per person) but there's no better restaurant, and it's a performance in several acts.

And just opposite, the best ice-cream parlour in town, **Le Glacier du Roi**, with a preference for fruit sorbets (we've never tasted such good kiwi, pear or peach flavours) or mint-chocolate and rum-raisin ice creams. Moreish!

CHEZ MICHEL
6, RUE DES CATALANS
13007 MARSEILLE

+334 91 52 64 22
restaurant-michel-13.fr

LE GLACIER DU ROI
39, RUE PAPETY
13007 MARSEILLE

leglacierduroi.com
Also at:
4, place Lenche, 13002 Marseille

THE INTERVIEW

- CLARA MARTOT BACRY -
JOURNALIST FOR MARSACTU.FR
AND CREATOR OF THE KEBAB CUP

Your favourite spot in Marseille?
I love going down the Canebière during the day. I live in Les Réformés and work at the Old Port. It's a trip I make every day by tram, but for me a successful weekend is one where I take time to stroll down the Canebière. This mix of people, this hyper-warm side that you don't find in many big cities ... Huveaune beach I also love, especially out of season, with surfers there and those immense spaces.

Where do you like to eat late at night?
I'm very faithful to Ashourya, a Syrian eatery at Cours Julien, open seven days a week and not closing until 11pm. Whatever you fancy or whatever your problem, you can go there, there'll always be someone around. The

number of times I've left the courthouse at 9.30 on a Monday evening and there was this beam of light in the night ...
I usually take a chicken sandwich with a very garlicky sauce. Otherwise, through the Kebab Cup (a competition to discover the best kebab in Marseille), I visited Avenue de Saint-Antoine, actually very central though when in the city centre you have the impression that it's far away. I also say central because you can live independently, absolutely everything is there and, unlike the Canebière which lacks life of an evening, you'll come across plenty of restaurants and a succession of quality brands.
I particularly like Kardeşler: you arrive at this restaurant, it's hyper-serious, huge, packed on Saturdays, carpets covering the walls and even the tables, you no longer feel at all as if you're in Marseille. And above all you're welcomed as if in a gourmet Turkish restaurant while you eat a kebab, with very well-cooked meat and an excellent homemade white sauce.

And after the restaurant, where to go?

L'Unic Bar, Cours Jean Ballard, open 8am to 4am every day except Sunday! The story goes that this and the Catalans Welcome café are the only two bars in the city that still have this permission to stay open until morning. An ex-prostitute launched this place. When you don't know what to do at the Old Port after midnight and don't want to be shut up in a nightclub, it's perfect, especially since there's a good kebab place opposite – Violettes. Unic is the only bar where I've ever sat alone at the counter, talking to strangers. The warmth and history of the place make it a neighbourhood must-see.

L'INSTAGRAM DE CLARA :
@marseillemondial

> *For me a successful weekend is one where I take time to stroll down the Canebière.*

THE BEST RESTAURANT IN THE SOUTH?

There's more to Marseille than bouillabaisse (which is actually a coastal dish and not unique to the city, but that's another story). Yet Marseille's other emblematic recipe has faded into obscurity over time: *pieds et paquets*, more commonly known as *pieds paquets*, made with mutton or lamb tripe and steamed potatoes. It takes around ten hours to prepare this iconic Marseille dish, and significant skill is required to cut the tripe with a 'buttonhole' so it can be stuffed and rolled into little bundles.

LA BONNE BRISE
1600, AVENUE DE PROVENCE
13170 LES PENNES-MIRABEAU

+334 42 02 60 89

According to the experts (and we agree), the queen of this culinary art is Suzy, who runs the restaurant La Bonne Brise, which has been in business just outside the city for forty years, against a backdrop of pretty olive trees. And it's not just her 'trotter packages' that deserve a look; the whole menu does, with a special mention for typical dishes like *alouettes sans tête* (literally 'headless larks': beef roulades stuffed with *petit salé* – salted pork – garlic and parsley, served with fresh pasta) and *bocconcini* (meat rolls stuffed with ham and cheese).

As a hostess, Suzy is unmatched – from the moment you step through the door. Rumour has it that a Michelin-starred chef once knelt before her after the meal, declaring that La Bonne Brise was 'the best restaurant in the South'.

ALL OF PROVENCE
IN A LITTLE-KNOWN MUSEUM

Tourists rarely venture to the village-like district of Château-Gombert on the outskirts of Marseille. Yet in 2023 the Musée Provençal, which has been around since 1928, reopened its newly restored doors to showcase 'domestic life, popular arts and traditions in Provence from Louis XIV to the present day'.

The museum's surprisingly young curator, Alexandre Mahue, offers guided tours, and his expertise is unsurpassed: nobody can explain Europe's largest collection of nativity scenes and figurines – known as *santons* – which totals nearly 4,000 pieces, better than him. He guides you from one room to the next, revealing treasures like the tea service once owned by writer Frédéric Mistral, a recreated Provençal kitchen and old wooden 'baguettes' engraved with the names of both the baker and the customer – from back in the day when Marseille's bakeries kept track of loyal customers' visits so they wouldn't have to pay each time. This journey back in time is an absolute must.

MUSÉE PROVENÇAL
5, PLACE DES HÉROS
13013 MARSEILLE

+334 91 68 14 38

museeprovencal.com
Instagram: @musee.provencal

THE MARSEILLAIS ALSO LOVE **WHIPPED CREAM AND RED MEAT**

People think the Marseillais love olive oil. And they do. But they're also crazy about cream, as evidenced by a century-old shop called **Le Royaume de la Chantilly** – literally 'the kingdom of whipped cream'. You should see the the long queues for this delicacy – which tastes almost caramelised here – at weekends. You'll be drooling over the salad bowls heaped with whipped cream while eyeing the various plastic tubs (100, 250 or 500 grams), which the sales assistant will wrap in white paper and tie with a blue ribbon. Serve it with *chouquettes* or seasonal strawberries – both also available here.

LE ROYAUME DE LA CHANTILLY
royaume-chantilly.com

Sébastopol shop
2, rue Granoux
13004 Marseille
+334 26 85 08 17

Saint-Barnabé shop
24, rue du Docteur Cauvin
13012 Marseille
+334 91 49 24 70

Le Redon shop
11, boulevard Redon
13009 Marseille
+334 91 25 66 61

And for those who think Marseille is only about seafood, think again: the city is actually teeming with carnivores, especially at **Bouillon**, a cheerful modern bistro in an up-and-coming neighbourhood. Here, the young Breton chef Auregan cooks up fantastic, creative dishes that are 100% meat. She also had the excellent idea of opening a shop next door that sells *pâtés en croute* (pâtés baked in a pastry crust) and homemade sausages.

BOUILLON
67, BOULEVARD CHAVE
13005 MARSEILLE

+334 91 67 30 10

bouillon-marseille.com
Instagram: @bouillon_marseille

JUICE FROM
A LEGENDARY
LOCAL KIOSK

'*Uvale*' stations (from the Latin *uva*, meaning grape), created in the 1930s, were once popular places serving grape juice. Though they've fallen out of fashion and disappeared over time, there's still one in France: in Marseille, opposite the Palais de Justice.

Yannis, who bears a striking resemblance to the award-winning actor Tahar Rahim, left the ready-to-wear business and the family auto shop to take over the kiosk, which was previously run by his aunt and uncle. Like them, he sources the grapes for his juice from Jacques, a grower near Avignon, from late July to late October. For the rest of the year customers can enjoy fresh-squeezed juices, always a blend of two fruits (orange, banana, strawberry, peach, pineapple and more), served in a glass or double glass.

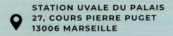

STATION UVALE DU PALAIS
27, COURS PIERRE PUGET
13006 MARSEILLE

Instagram: @ stationuvaledupalais

THE BEST PICNIC
IN TOWN

Chef Pierre Giannetti was a key figure in Marseille's culinary scene during the 2010s with Le Grain de Sel, which was named 'Best Bistro in France' by Le Fooding guide in 2012. In 2017, he left behind his traditional restaurant to launch a catering service with his partners Marine and Sandi.

La Fabriquerie, as it's called, is exceptionally good, serving up restaurant-quality dishes in takeaway trays. Everything here is pure gold: potato salad that's like mashed potatoes but better, dangerously addictive brownies by the slice, strawberries in passion-fruit syrup and pistou soup, to name just a few of the options.

For lunch, you can either eat right there (if you arrive early, as there are only eight seats at the table), or get a takeaway and enjoy it on the beach, just 500 metres away!

 LA FABRIQUERIE
71, AVENUE DE LA CORSE
13007 MARSEILLE

+337 67 17 35 95

Instagram: @lafabriquerie.marseille

DIVE INTO
THE STOREROOMS
OF THE MUCEM

Everyone knows the Museum of European and Mediterranean Civilizations (Mucem), but have you heard of its little brother? The Centre de Conservation et de Ressources (CCR; Conservation and Resource Centre) houses the roughly 250,000 objects, 350,000 photographs, 150,000 books, and 200,000 posters, prints and postcards that the Mucem draws on for its new exhibitions. These collections themselves come from the Musée de l'Homme (Museum of Humanity) and the Musée National des Arts et Traditions Populaires (National Museum of Popular Arts and Traditions).

On the first Tuesday of each month, visitors can join a 90-minute tour of the centre (reservations required), which was designed by architect Corinne Vezzoni. When asked which object from the collections moved her most, she mentioned the many ribbons marked with the names and birthdates of abandoned children, as well as the range of traditional garments worn at key life ceremonies (weddings, funerals, etc.) across various Mediterranean countries.

 CENTRE DE CONSERVATION ET DE RESSOURCES DU MUCEM
1, RUE CLOVIS HUGUES
13003 MARSEILLE

+334 84 35 14 23

reservationccr@mucem.org
mucem.org

ART
BY APPOINTMENT

Despite its proximity to Le Corbusier's Cité Radieuse ('Radiant City'), the Mazargues district remains relatively unknown. Yet it is here that Emmanuelle Luciani chose to convert her 19th-century ancestral home into a gallery and artists' residence: Pavillon Southway.

An exhibition curator and artist in her own right, Emmanuelle Luciani is a key figure in the local cultural scene and beyond, also serving as the artistic director of the Artists' Residencies programme of the Fondation d'entreprise Hermès. Guided tours of the Pavillon Southway, a Marseille landmark, and the deliberately anachronistic works it houses, are available by appointment (5 euros per person). Bonus: the building doubles as a bed and breakfast – expect to pay 130 euros for a 'night at the museum'.

PAVILLON SOUTHWAY
433, BOULEVARD MICHELET
13009 MARSEILLE

hello@southwaystudio.com
southwaystudio.com

Guided tour: €5/person
Overnight stay: approx. €130

MARSEILLE, PIZZA CAPITAL OF FRANCE

It's a national and weekly pastime: eating pizza, or rather 'pizz' as it's called in Marseille. In fact, pizza first arrived in France here, at the very end of the 19th century, brought by workers from the Naples region. Since then, Marseille has become the pizza capital of France. It's home to two establishments that opened in the 1940s and are still going strong today: Chez Sauveur and, our favourite, Chez Étienne. Here you can enjoy authentic Marseille-style pizza, characterised by burnt edges, Emmental instead of mozzarella, and *moitié-moitié* ('half and half') pies, with tomato and cheese on one side and tomato and anchovies on the other. Marseille is also the birthplace of the famous pizza truck, invented here in the early 1960s.

> The iconic pizzeria: More than just a restaurant, **Chez Étienne** is a landmark you must visit at least once. In this 'pizzaria', the staff greets you like old friends, even if they've never seen you before ('*Ça va les chéris?*' – 'Everything good, loves?'). Start with the famous fried *supions* (small cuttlefish) with greens in a salad bowl, then move on to the pizza, a prime example of the

CHEZ ÉTIENNE
43, RUE DE LORETTE
13002 MARSEILLE

+336 16 39 78 73

Marseille style, served by the slice or with a knife and fork. Many people also order meat, but you can simply round off your meal with the wood-fired apple tart with vanilla ice cream.

> The pizzeria hidden behind a bar: The affable Andrea, a true Neapolitan, is at the helm of **Trattoria Partenope**, this relatively new restaurant located at the back of a local bar and decorated with old press clippings about various events (the police station is just across the street). We especially love the pizza with octopus ragout and the classic margherita.

> The best pizza truck in Marseille: La Blancarde may not be Marseille's most central district (though geographically, it kind of is), but when it comes to pizza trucks, it's all about the people – and **Gérald Oliveri**'s is our favourite. It feels like it's been there for ever, a true neighbourhood landmark, serving up huge pizzas by the slice (around 2 euros a 'portion', as locals like to say). And the man who makes them is an actual, bona fide chef, who might even share stories about his past with another Gérald, the 3-star chef at Le Petit Nice...

> Marseille's favourite guilty pleasure: You can also grab pizza from the bakery, where it's usually rectangular and brioche-like. One of our favourite local bakeries for pizza is **La Fournée de Lodi**. Another great option is Mando, near the city's most central beach, Catalans, which serves triangular portions with slightly underbaked dough that makes them especially addictive.

TRATTORIA PARTENOPE
56, RUE DE L'ÉVÊCHÉ
13002 MARSEILLE

+334 91 91 22 00
trattoria-partenope.fr
Instagram: @trattoria._partenope

CHEZ GÉ (PIZZA TRUCK)
93, BOULEVARD
DE LA BLANCARDE
13004 MARSEILLE

+336 48 03 90 97

CHEZ GÉ

© AGATHE HERNANDEZ

📍 **LA FOURNÉE DE LODI**
1, RUE D'ALGER
13006 MARSEILLE

+334 91 42 67 86

79

THE INTERVIEW

- MÉDÉRIC GASQUET-CYRUS -
LINGUIST SPECIALISING IN MARSEILLES VERNACULAR

Your favourite place in town?
The Velodrome stadium. Since 1992, I've been a member of the Virage Sud club and when I go in there, climb the steps and see the green lawns as I did the first time, I say to myself: 'This is it, I'm home.' There's something going on ... With the Ultras, we're familiar with victories and defeats – some folk you hug as if they were friends when you don't even know their names. At 9pm the match starts but we meet up with friends at 6pm for at least two happy hours of aperitifs, at the Napo snackbar on Prado roundabout. One comes with tapenade, another with aioli, yet another with baguette. We're brought things to eat but must pay 50 or 60 euros for the drink (a bottle of *pastis*).

One word to describe Marseille?
Rebelle: even if overworked to death, I see no other adjectives that better characterise the city, because

we always have this 'we are against' side, including things that we make ourselves. There is also *oaï* (pronounce '*ouaille*'), meaning bordel or mess. It sounds good, it's native Neapolitan. But you can have good and bad *oaï*. The bad is when you're stuck in traffic or there's trash cans on the street. When you put *oaï* in the stadium or a concert was *oaï*, that's the opposite, a good thing. This word is great because of its many meanings, you can do plenty with it.

A word or expression you can no longer stand?

'*Marseille baby*'. At first this was the equivalent of '*on craint dégun*' ('we're afraid of nobody') in a modern version, the Jul rapper age. But this expression has become so well known throughout France that, more and more, the people who use it are no longer Marseillais, but those who just want to be like them and find it cool to say such a thing. Where it bothers me most of all is when used to justify the unjustifiable. Such as when we see youngsters *wheeling* (riding a bike on the back wheel) or burning pedestrian crossings, we'll say 'it's Marseille baby'. But that doesn't make me laugh. I love my city but don't want to justify everything. Now 'Marseille baby' is becoming a kind of warning.

An out-of-date expression you still like?

My grandmother used to talk about the *mounguis*. 'Hey, pal, what're we eating tonight? – *mounguis*!' It means 'nothing'. We say that for fun. I like it because there's this sound effect, we don't even know where it comes from but then, we chatter mea-ninglessly. Marseille gives you the pleasure of free speech. We like to talk. Moreover, although the city has changed a lot in terms of image or economy, it's kept its spirit: the Marseillais always speak to others on the street, there's always this neighbourhood life.

> *Marseille gives you the pleasure of free speech.*

THE INTERVIEW

LUNCH
AT THE FARM

There was a time, not so long ago, when Marseille was virtually self-sufficient agriculturally speaking. While those days are over, some urban farms remain as a reminder of just how sprawling the city is. These farms do more than just produce food. Take **Le Talus**, for example, a project run by the Heko Farm association. Easily accessible by bus, it features a garden, henhouse and fields where vegetables and herbs are grown without chemicals on an 800-square-metre plot. When it's open (usually Wednesday and/or Saturday mornings), you can pick your own produce and enjoy a reasonably priced drink or organic vegan meal.

📍 **LE TALUS**
603 ('LE JARDIN') + 623 ('LE VILLAGE')
RUE SAINT-PIERRE
13012 MARSEILLE

+334 91 47 48 72
letalus.com / contact@heko.farm
Instagram: @letalusmarseille

📍 **ROCKETTE**
81, TRAVERSE DE LA FONTAINE
13014 MARSEILLE

20 euros per person
Instagram: @rockette_marseille

We also love the roof terrace, with its panoramic view of the towers of the Air Bel housing estate and the hills of Saint Cyr. Be sure to check out the extensive cultural programme – concerts, shows, workshops, and more – on their website and social media channels.

Another urban farm worth mentioning is **Rockette**, which offers themed walks and introductory courses in wild fruit picking.

A MEAL
IN THE CALANQUES

This restaurant may be called Le Château, but it isn't a palace at all. The name is simply what local fishermen called the large summer bastide – much bigger than their cabins – back in the late 1940s. The Rambaldy family has been running the place for more than 40 years, and now Sébastien is in charge. He hasn't just recruited cheerful waiters; he also oversees the cooking, which ranges from homemade *panisses* (chickpea flour fritters) to rich *brousse* (a type of fresh cheese) and pesto ravioli gratin, not to mention an unusual sea urchin flan with a coulis of *favouilles*, small crabs from Marseille.

N.B. Even when the Calanques are closed to cars in fine weather, you can still drive to the restaurant – just be sure to inform Le Château of your number plate in advance.

 LE CHÂTEAU SORMIOU
ROUTE DU FEU DE LA CALANQUE DE SORMIOU
13009 MARSEILLE

From April to July and from September to October | +334 91 25 08 69 | lechateausormiou.fr
Instagram: @lechateausormiou

HIKE UP TO THE MOST **BEAUTIFUL VANTAGE POINT IN THE CALANQUES**

The **Calanque de Sugiton** is undoubtedly one of the most beautiful coves in Marseille. Reaching a height of 245 metres, the lookout point of the same name offers a breathtaking panoramic view of Sugiton cove below, Mont Puget and Morgiou cove to the right.

Reaching this former military lookout requires less athleticism than descending to the cove itself, and almost anyone can do it (allow 35 to 40 minutes for the hike). From the Luminy car park, take the first path (which marks the beginning of every hike from here), and after about half an hour turn right at the crossroads to walk the final 10-minute stretch.

LA CALANQUE DE SUGITON
LUMINY CAR PARK OR
LUMINY – PN DES CALANQUES STATION
13009 MARSEILLE

To limit erosion from overcrowding, access to the cove is by reservation only during the summer months, so be sure to check the national park website in advance

calanques-parcnational.fr

BAIN DES DAMES BEACH

Take your time to admire the view and snap some pictures, then retrace your steps a few hundred metres and sit among the rocks just to the right of the path, slightly out of the way. It's a great spot to enjoy breakfast (if you're coming by direct bus from Castellane station, stop by the excellent Maison Saint-Honoré bakery for some of their famous flavoured brioche rolls) or simply relax with a drink.

For more experienced hikers or lovers of less-frequented trails, the intersection at the end of the first trail gives access to many other hiking routes: Mont Puget by Col Ricard, Calanque de Morgiou by the Sentier Noir, Col de la Candelle and Pas de l'Oeil de Verre (beware: dizzy heights!).

As far as beaches go we love **Bain des Dames**, a sandy beach reached by a short drive from the city centre. Charming, with its huts in the background.

Further away and quieter, the pebbled **cove of Figuerolles** is a cinematic setting approached from above, down the steps.

COVE OF FIGUEROLLES

HIGH-FLYING
DRINKS SCENE

The motto of **Bar Gaspard**, a signature cocktail bar loved by local lawyers? 'Laissez-nous faire' ('Just leave it to us'). Benjamin Colombani takes care of everything – an ace shaker who learned at London's prestigious Connaught hotel – and makes low-sugar drinks that often include mezcal (agave spirit). But the star cocktail is *Concombre masqué* (gin, cucumber, basil, Sichuan pepper and a little green cardamom essence), spicy and fresh, giving this impression of drinking detox juice ... but better. We also love the Copperbay, another mixologie hotspot.

BAR GASPARD
7, BOULEVARD NOTRE-DAME
13006 MARSEILLE

+336 88 23 86 66
Instagram: @bargaspard
Cocktails around 12 euros

APOTEK
2, RUE CONSOLAT
13001 MARSEILLE

+336 32 10 48 17

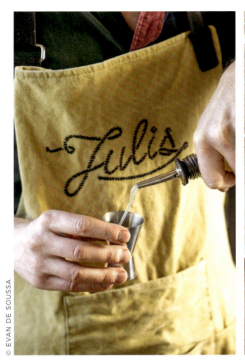

For a taste of paradise, head for **Julis**. A garden within a garden – in this case Parc Puget – just below Notre-Dame-de-la-Garde. The type of place where we'd like to spend every weekend, because it has everything – the barbecue smell from the summer kitchen, a superb view over the city and port (complete with sunset) and tables set up near the veg garden. And the expertise of Thibaut Dropsy, a 30-something expert in high-end, luxury bars. As Julis is dedicated to cocktails and tapas, we could equally well start the evening at its big-brother neighbour, Sépia, run by chef Paul Langlère, a Marseillais from the kitchens of Plaza Athénée hotel.

Also worth exploring: **Carry Nation**, a fake soapmaker that gives way to a real cocktail bar where you can sip a 'Ramos gin fizz', a creamy drink made from gin, juice of yellow and green lemons, crème fraîche, egg white and orange-blossom syrup, dreamed up by Guillaume Ferroni (a key figure in Marseille indie distilleries) and his team.

Lovers of fine seasoned liquids can also turn to **Apotek**, a tiny pastel-coloured counter in the Réformés district at the top of the Canebière. The cocktails are poured into antique glasses and one of the star drinks is Abuelita, with its smoky taste, prepared with tequila, mezcal, honey, turmeric and lime.

JULIS
2, RUE VAUVENARGUES
13007 MARSEILLE

+337 62 26 55 86
Instagram: @sepia13007
Cocktails around 12 euros,
dishes around 11 euros

CARRY NATION
SECRET ADDRESS
13006 MARSEILLE

+339 50 26 01 66
Address revealed when booking at:
carrynation.fr

THE INTERVIEW

- AUDREY EMERY -
FOUNDER OF LA LAITERIE MARSEILLAISE

La Laiterie is the only dairy in the city to make its own cheeses, right in the centre. Customer favourites?
Saint-Victor, a goat cheese with a frothy texture at the core, it's very comforting. In winter, there's *crottin de vache* with timut pepper and notes of citrus, which enhances the flavour of a rather sweet cheese. I'm also thinking of *halloum* (from *halloumi*, a compressed block originally from Cyprus, usually made with sheep's or goat's milk, sometimes cow's). We're the only ones in Marseille to make them ourselves, otherwise there's only the mass-produced vacuum-packed version, quite bland. Not to mention our Marseille blue cheeses, rather a challenge, with a pleasant tang, not too salty either.

How do you see the city evolving, speaking as someone born here?
After 2013, when Marseille was European Capital of Culture, something happened. I saw

people's eyes change expression when I talked about our city elsewhere. There really was a turnabout at that point. I remember when I was little and we wanted to eat out, there wasn't much choice. Since five, ten years, there's much more on offer, more modern. Before, there were *fricasses* (Tunisian fried pastry with assorted filling) and Italian dishes, we didn't leave the Mediterranean. Today we do, and if there's a Mediterranean dish on the plate, we're not scared to push it away!

After 2013, when Marseille was European Capital of Culture, something happened.

A souvenir to take home?

Le Sérail stain remover soap stick. It costs 2 euros and with its added bicarbonate I tell you it removes anything. Various retailers sell it, including the pharmacy next door, as well as the workshop-boutique at Sainte-Marthe in the 14th district. For an edible souvenir, on the other hand, I love the long *orangettes* coated in dark chocolate from Chocolaterie de Puyricard on Avenue du Prado. Or the fruit pasta from Nouchig (a downtown establishment known for its chocolate dragees). Or the chocolate-coated frozen chestnuts from La Baleine à Cabosse, which works directly with cocoa beans ...

The city borders on the Mediterranean and yet it's not so easy to find good fish ...

True, there's not many fish shops or first-class fish restaurants in the city. People forget that Marseille is a working-class city and fish is expensive. At the Au Bout du quai restaurant, near the town hall, they offer fine local and fresh fish-based dishes, including bouillabaisse for 36 euros. Other than that the Poissonnerie du Golf comes to mind. They've been there for a while, quite a few restaurants use them.

LA LAITERIE MARSEILLAISE
86, rue Sainte
13007 Marseille
+334 91 06 73 82
Instagram: @lalaiteriemarseillaise

TASTE THE OVERSEAS **TERRITORIES**

Marseille the 'land of welcome' is no mere cliché: this is a city where you can find authentic home cooking from all the French overseas territories ...

> Take **Doumé / La Corsoise** (yes, it has two names), a Corsican canteen that's been bustling every lunchtime since 1975, often full of taxi drivers and doctors – generally a very good sign for a restaurant. It's run by an old Corsican lady (the famous 'Corsoise' whom everyone calls Nénette) and her son Dominique (known as Doumé). The menu includes veal cannelloni and creamy gnocchi au gratin, prepared by the Kabyle chef, who also makes tagines and couscous. There's also excellent *brocciu* (fresh cheese) mousse, topped with a clementine coulis.

LA CORSOISE
29, RUE DÉSIRÉE-CLARY
13002 MARSEILLE

+334 91 90 40 88

LES DÉLICES-PÂTISSERIE D'AIX

> Despite the city's considerable Algerian community, good couscous is surprisingly hard to find in Marseille. However, there's a little street in the city centre – one that even most locals don't know – where you can sample regional Kabyle or Berber specialities, as smoke billows from the barbecue. At **Tella**, choose whatever dish catches your eye (grilled sheep's head or sardines in harissa sauce?) and the waiter will generously fill your plate.

> Visiting **Les Délices-Pâtisserie d'Aix**, a veritable Ali Baba's cave of Middle Eastern and Maghreb desserts since 1978, is a must if you have a sweet tooth. It's like stepping into a café in Sidi Bou Saïd. Order tea with pine nuts or café au lait, and surrender to the vast array of pastries: honey doughnuts, loukoum, *montécaos*, *makroud*, *zlabia* …

TELLA 10, RUE DE LA FARE 13001 MARSEILLE	LES DÉLICES-PÂTISSERIE D'AIX 1, RUE NATIONALE 13001 MARSEILLE
+337 86 32 46 21	+334 91 90 12 50

CELEBRATING **THE SEA**

To experience the famous '*Oursinades*' (from the French word for sea urchin, *oursin*), you'll need to be in Marseille on one of the first three Sundays in February – or rather, 30 kilometres to the west, in the town of Carry-le-Rouet, which has been hosting this event for decades. Here, you can buy fresh sea urchins, oysters, squid, sardines and cuttlefish from the stalls before sitting down at one of the communal tables. Some people bring their own wine, bread and condiments. The event officially starts at 10am, but it's best to arrive early to make sure you find a spot.

Jonas Bizord and Damien Féraud, two of the last sea-urchin fishermen in the Marseille area, recommend the fluorescent orange gonads (the edible part of the sea urchin), claiming that they're 'really very sweet'. A word of advice: take the scenic train ride along what's known as the '*Côte Bleue*' ('Blue Coast').

N.B. Several neighbouring towns also host their own *Oursinades*: Sausset-les-Pins in January and Fos-sur-Mer in March.

 PORT DE CARRY-LE-ROUET
QUAI À FOUQUE
13620 CARRY-LE-ROUET

otcarrylerouet.fr/fr/se-divertir-et-bouger/grandes-manifestations/191-les-oursinades

FAÏENCE
IN A MUSEUM

Joseph Clérissy, Gaspard Robert, Honoré Savy, Antoine Bonnefoy, 'Veuve Perrin' … While these names may not mean much to you today, in the 17th and 18th centuries they were the leading figures in Marseille tableware – masters of faïence (earthenware), a type of ceramic. The city even became the international capital of faïence between 1750 and 1789 – so it's not surprising that the immense collection of the famous Metropolitan Museum in New York includes pieces from Marseille.

Closer to home, the Château Borély has housed the Musée des Arts Décoratifs, de la Faïence et de la Mode (Museum of Decorative Arts, Earthenware and Fashion) since 2013. Showcasing artisans skilled in these arts, as well as exhibits of furniture, tapestries and designs by the great couturiers, it's a museum you'll fall in love with.

CHÂTEAU BORÉLY
132, AVENUE CLOT-BEY
13008 MARSEILLE

+334 91 55 33 60
chateau-borely-musee@marseille.fr

Free first Sunday of month

© MDM DAVID GIANCATARINA

HEAD OUT TO MEET SOME **STREET VENDORS**

Marseille is all about street snacks. Here are three examples to prove it.

> **Papa Omri's magic cart**: Belkacem Omri, known as Papa Omri, is a local living legend with his 'all-music magic cart', set up at the foot of the Mucem (Museum of European and Mediterranean Civilizations: see p. 68). In fact, Mucem has even bought one of his carts to keep in its reserve collection. Between May and September, the retired Tunisian sells mint and pine nut tea, cold drinks, peanuts and pralines to the locals. There's even a playlist on Spotify if you want to hear the music Papa Omri plays.

LE CHARIOT DE PAPA OMRI
AT THE FOOT OF THE MUCEM
7, PROMENADE ROBERT LAFFONT
13002 MARSEILLE

From May to September

© AGATHE HERNANDEZ

> **Charlie's roasted chestnuts**: Raphaël Cocozza, a Corsican going on 70, has been running this roasted chestnut stand for over 20 years. It might not seem like it, but he's a softie at heart, and if he takes a shine to you, he'll tell you all about his old life as a dock worker in the port – while doling out portions of hot chestnuts (3.50 euros for a bag of about 15 to 19). Raphaël has a strong physique: he's on his feet all day, shovelling large scoops of chestnuts into the old oven (which heats up to 200 degrees Celsius), sweeping the floor and moving around bags and canisters. The tradition dates back to 1950, when the Gueit family and the Charlie Marrons company invented locomotive-shaped roasting stations to attract passers-by.

> **Cocoman's sorbet**: It's all a matter of luck – you never know on which Marseille beach you'll find Christophe Martinez, aka Cocoman, the artisan coconut sorbet maker and seller, wearing dungarees and a hat. What's certain is that he'll be somewhere starting in April, and that he pours his heart into preparing his ice cream using coconut milk, sweetened condensed milk, cinnamon, nutmeg, vanilla, almonds and lime zest in wooden buckets that weigh over 17 kilos.

IN THE FOOTSTEPS OF **MARCEL PAGNOL**

The year 2024 marked the 50th anniversary of the death of this native of the region, writer and brilliant filmmaker (*The Baker's Wife, César, Marius, Le schpountz, Fanny* – to name just a few of his films). To pay tribute to him, head for **Château de la Buzine**, a Louis XIII-style castle he acquired in the 1940s with the aim of turning it into his 'Cité du Cinéma'. A free exhibition explores the history of the man, as well as the characters that fascinated him.

Pagnol is buried in the nearby cemetery, where his epitaph reads that he 'loved springs, his friends and his wife'. After paying your respects, take a walk through the picturesque village of La Treille, now part of Marseille, before grabbing a bite to eat at **Le Cigalon** (a nod to one of Pagnol's works, of course). Here, enjoy Provençal specialities served by the charming staff and the even more impressive view from the terrace.

CHÂTEAU DE LA BUZINE
56, TRAVERSE DE LA BUZINE
13011 MARSEILLE

+334 91 14 51 80
labuzine.com
Instagram: @chateaudelabuzine

LE CIGALON (LA TREILLE)
9, BOULEVARD LOUIS PASTEUR
13011 MARSEILLE

+334 91 34 36 09
cigalon-latreille.fr

ROOMS
WITH A VIEW

One of the great pleasures of life is obviously to sleep directly over the sea. And preferably without even having to cross the road.

Luckily Marseille has three good addresses, a little expensive but the perfect location comes at a price.

> **Les Bords de Mer**: this 19-room hotel is ideally located, halfway between the Old Port and the rocky beach of Malmousque. The name is perfectly chosen as Catalans beach is directly below. Luxury hotel group Domaines de Fontenille is behind the modern development, which was inaugurated in the spirit of the 1950s in late 2018. There is a spa, a rooftop bar and a restaurant on the ground floor.

 LES BORDS DE MER
52, CORNICHE PRÉSIDENT JOHN F. KENNEDY
13007 MARSEILLE

+334 13 94 34 00   Instagram : @lesbordsdemer

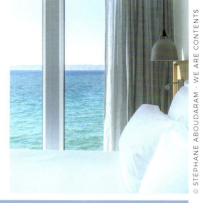

© RICHARD D'HAUGHTON

> **Le Petit Nice**: lair of chef Gérald Passedat, the first to earn the city three Michelin stars in 2008. But there's not only the great restaurant, there's also a Relais & Châteaux hotel overlooking the renowned rocky beach of Malmousque (Fausse Monnaie cove to be exact). Undoubtedly the most beautiful in all Marseille, designed by star architect Rudy Ricciotti for the opening of the Mucem.

 LE PETIT NICE
17 RUE DES BRAVES (ANSE DE MALDORMÉ)
13007 MARSEILLE

+334 91 59 25 92

passedat.fr
Instagram: @lepetitnicepassedat

> **Tuba Club**: the word 'tuba' is no longer associated only with the tube of a diving mask but with this small luxury hotel opened in 2020 in Les Goudes, a dream port still anchored in Marseille but at the far end, the Mediterranean a very close neighbour. This was the stronghold of diving pro Jacques Mayol. Interior designer Marion Mailaender, in great demand these days, has created (small) rooms that look like modern cabins; but there are also more spacious places to stay known as 'villas'.

TUBA CLUB
2, BOULEVARD ALEXANDRE DELABRE
13008 MARSEILLE

+334 91 25 13 16
Instagram: @tuba.club

Minimum stay of two nights
Ask for rooms 3 and 4, as they are not adjacent to the restaurant terrace

DISCOVER
A LITTLE-KNOWN ISLAND

Frioul and the Château d'If? Why not set sail instead for the lesser-known island of Degaby? Built by Louis XIV to defend the harbour of Marseille, the island was later sold to a wealthy timber merchant and industrialist, who gifted it to his wife Liane Degaby. A famous music-hall performer of the Belle Époque, she hosted extravagant parties here for the haute bourgeoisie.

The island recently opened to the public, and a short boat trip will get you there for lunch or dinner. Once there, you have two options: the restaurant (expect to pay 50 to 60 euros *à la carte*) or the bar area with deckchairs, where you can enjoy more casual, yet still beautifully prepared food – thanks to chef Sébastien Dugast, a veteran of the 3-star Michelin restaurant Le Petit Nice.

An insider tip? Aim for lunch so you can spend the whole afternoon soaking up the sun and, above all, swimming amongst the rocks, with the place basically to yourself.

ÎLE DEGABY
15 MIN FROM QUAI DU MUCEM
13002 MARSEILLE

From May to October | iledegaby.com | 20 euros per person for return boat trip
Add to that the restaurant meal or drinks at the bar

MARSEILLE'S
MOST BEAUTIFUL VIEW

Everyone in Marseille knows chef Gérald Passedat's Le Petit Nice (see p. 116). You need to be swimming in cash to treat yourself to the bouillabaisse menu (400 euros per person). But what not everyone knows (including many locals!) is that the same location is home to a much more affordable bistro, Le 19-17, named after the date the Passedat family bought the building. The *petits farcis provençaux* (Provençal stuffed vegetables) are exquisite, the vanilla *vacherin* (meringue ice cream cake) is one of the best around and, to top it all off, the view over the Mediterranean is the same as from its Michelin-starred neighbour: the most beautiful in Marseille.

Almost all year round, guests are seated on the terrace – unlike those at the gourmet restaurant.

 LE 19-17
17, RUE DES BRAVES (ANSE DE MALDORMÉ)
13007 MARSEILLE

+334 91 59 25 92
passedat.fr

The bistro car park is reserved for guests of Le Petit Nice and the hotel

ACKNOWLEDGEMENTS

Thanks to **CHARLOTTE BRUNET**, creator of experiences around the Pavillon Southway and the Mucem collections, as well as **CHARLOTTE VILLEDIEU**, valued friend behind the urban farm and the trail to Sugiton belvedere, for their contributions. Not to mention **OPHÉLIE FRANCQ**, who has a way with words when it comes to cocktails.

Thanks to the awesome duo from **CAGNARD** studio (but not only there), **AGATHE HERNANDEZ** and **MERIADEC MALLAT**, for their pictures with sunshine and smiles at heart. Thanks to **AGATHE RABIN** for immortalising two monuments of the 7th arrondissement.

Thanks to **MARIANNE TIBERGHIEN**, good fairy of Marseille Centre, whose unexpected meetings and phone calls are always enlightening.

Thanks to **VÉRONIQUE**, **ALEX**, **CÉCILE** and **PHILIPPE** for being around.

Thanks to **VALENTINE**, for our hundreds of Marseille experiences together and for even more to come!

Thanks to **SOLAL**, my (almost) favourite Marseillais.

This book was created by:
Ezéchiel Zérah, author
Emmanuelle Willard Toulemonde, layout
Sophie Schlondorff and Caroline Lawrence, translation
Sonny Alexander, editing
Jana Gough, proofreading
Thomas Jonglez, Morgane De Wulf and Mado de La Quintinie, publishing

Map p. 10-11 : © Sacha Doubroff
Cover photo: © Sergii Figurnyi – stock.adobe.com
Back cover' illustrations: © Mvezo Karamchand Hay – © tttboram – © Clker-Free-Vector-Images – © Katamaheen – © OpenClipart-Vectors – © Mudassar Iqbal – © Nina Garman – © Adobe Stock, Anastasiia

You can write to us at info@editionsjonglez.com
Follow us on Instagram: @editionsjonglez

THANK YOU

From the same publisher

Atlases

Atlas of extreme weather
Atlas of forbidden places
Atlas of geographical curiosities
Atlas of unusual wines

Photo Books

Abandoned America
Abandoned Asylums
Abandoned Australia
Abandoned Belgium
Abandoned Churches: Unclaimed places of worship
Abandoned cinemas of the world
Abandoned France
Abandoned Germany
Abandoned Italy
Abandoned Japan
Abandoned Lebanon
Abandoned Spain
Abandoned USSR
Abandoned world – An AI-generated exploration
After the Final Curtain – The Fall of the American Movie Theater
After the Final Curtain – America's Abandoned Theaters
Baikonur – Vestiges of the Soviet space programme
Cinemas – A French heritage
Clickbait – A visual journey through AI-generated stories
Destination Wellness – The 35 best places in the world to take time out
Forbidden France
Forbidden Places – Vol. 1
Forbidden Places – Vol. 2
Forbidden Places – Vol. 3
Forgotten Heritage
Oblivion
Secret sacred sites
Venice deserted
Venice from the skies

'Soul of' Guides

Soul of Amsterdam
Soul of Athens
Soul of Barcelona
Soul of Berlin
Soul of Bruxelles
Soul of Detroit
Soul of Kyoto
Soul of Lisbon
Soul of Los Angeles
Soul of Marrakesh
Soul of Milan
Soul of New York
Soul of Paris
Soul of Rome
Soul of Tokyo
Soul of Venice
Soul of Vienna

'Secret' Guides

Secret Amsterdam
Secret Bali
Secret Bangkok
Secret Barcelona
Secret Bath – An unusual guide
Secret Belfast
Secret Berlin
Secret Boston – An unusual guide
Secret Brighton – An unusual guide
Secret Brooklyn
Secret Brussels
Secret Budapest
Secret Buenos Aires
Secret Campania
Secret Cape Town
Secret Copenhagen
Secret Dublin – An unusual guide
Secret Edinburgh – An unusual guide
Secret Florence
Secret French Riviera
Secret Geneva
Secret Glasgow
Secret Granada
Secret Helsinki
Secret Istanbul
Secret Johannesburg
Secret Lisbon
Secret Liverpool – An unusual guide
Secret London – An unusual guide
Secret London – Unusual bars & restaurants
Secret Los Angeles
Secret Louisiana – An unusual guide
Secret Madrid
Secret Mexico City
Secret Milan
Secret Montreal – An unusual guide
Secret Naples
Secret New Orleans
Secret New York – An unusual guide
Secret New York – Curious activities
Secret New York – Hidden bars & restaurants

Secret Paris
Secret Prague
Secret Provence
Secret Rio
Secret Rome
Secret Seville
Secret Singapore
Secret Stockholm
Secret Sussex – An unusual guide
Secret Tokyo
Secret Tuscany
Secret Venice
Secret Vienna
Secret Washington D.C.
Secret York - An unusual guide

Follow us on Facebook and Instagram

In accordance with regularly upheld French jurisprudence (Toulouse 14-01-1887), the publisher will not be deemed responsible for any involuntary errors or omissions that may subsist in this guide despite our diligence and verifications by the editorial staff.

Any reproduction of the content, or part of the content, of this book by whatever means is forbidden without prior authorisation by the publisher.

© JONGLEZ 2025
Registration of copyright: May 2025 – Edition: 01
ISBN: 978-2-36195-829-9
Printed in Slovakia by Polygraf